"A" 22 & 23
Louis Zukofsky

GROSSMAN PUBLISHERS
A Division of The Viking Press
New York 1975

Copyright © 1973, 1974, 1975 by Louis Zukofsky
All rights reserved
First published in 1975 by Grossman Publishers
625 Madison Avenue, New York, N.Y. 10022
Published simultaneously in Canada by
The Macmillan Company of Canada Limited
Printed in U.S.A.
"A" 22, Part I and Part II, originally appeared in *Poetry*; a portion of *"A" 23* originally appeared in *The Transatlantic Review.*

Library of Congress Cataloging in Publication Data
Zukofsky, Louis, 1904-
   "A" 22 & 23.
   I. Title.
PS3549.U47A734   811'.5'2   75-17777
ISBN 0-670-00598-3

CANISIUS COLLEGE LIBRARY
BUFFALO, N. Y.

"A"–22

AN ERA
ANY TIME
OF YEAR

Others letters a sum owed
ages account years each year
out of old fields, permute
blow blue up against yellow
—scapes welcome young birds—initial

transmutes itself, swim near and
read a weed's reward—grain
an omen a good omen
the chill mists greet woods
ice, flowers—their soul's return

let me live here ever,
sweet now, silence foison to
on top of the weather
it has said it before
why that was you that

is how you weather division
a peacocks grammar perching—and
perhaps think that they see
or they fly thru a
window not knowing it there

the window could they sing
it broken need not bleed
one proof of its strength
a need birds cannot feign
persisting for flight as when

they began to exist—error
if error vertigo their sun
eyes delirium—both initial together

rove into the blue initial
surely it carves a breath

one air then a host
an air not my own
an earth of three trees
sleep revives—night adds hours
awake to augur days impend

the trumpet ice edges shrill,
twigged heart flounce the Land
be not fought—greatness remain
what avails the life to
leaf to flower to fruit

the season's colors a ripening
work their detail—the perennial
invariance won't hollow it, no
averaging makes their tones—Paradise
the swept brain blood warmer

leaving it eyes' heat stars'
dawn mirror to west window
binds the sun's east—steersman's
one guess at certainty made
with an assemblage of naught—

yet in cells not vacuum
recórds as tho horses rushed
definite as an aching nerve
pleads feed and feed back—
spine follows path once born,

to arrogate it small eloquence,
an affair with the moon
it looked as if it
looked up someway above earth
a hectic of an instant

until computed in the metal—
tidal waves also timing it
moon's day and earth's month
figured closer—blazed sun, white
under weightless dancing after the

predictable vaguer with time's increase,
seemed to say: the same
earth gaze returns to them
weightless, inkling of outlines, unearthing
always only their past futures

hearing iron horse scrape me
begging so to speak, stay—
history their figment of miracle—
young led, painting a standpipe
seeing it swan or stork—

fish purl in the weir:
we are caught by our
own knowing, barb yellow hard
ever yet—*oink* little jangler
thrums—sigh, prattle sea flood—

shard porcelain learned blue veined
by wreathed penny in ice—
coo (where?) dig or not
piece dig who with what
what with ninth year's gait

of eight, weird's lettered pebble
a pan plinth table of
law—noon wait a weight
wait it is very right,
sink killick read the kelp—

cherries, knave of a valentine,
were ever blue of yellow,
birds, harp in three trees—
now summer happy new year
any time of year—so

no piper lead with nonsense
before its music don't, horse,
brag of faith too much—
fear thawed reach three-fingered chord
sweet treble hold lovely—initial

Late later and much later
surge sea erupts boiling molten
lava island from ice, land
seen into color thru day
and night: voiced, once unheard
earth beginning idola of years
that love well forget late.
History's best emptied of names'
impertinence met on the ways:
shows then the little earth
at regard of the heavens
unfolding tract and flying congregate
birds their hiding valentine's day:
little horse can you speak
won't know till it speaks:
three birches in the meadow
kiss: constant please. Attentive as
good: no prophet no footnote:
earliest mountain the lowest the
seas moil, thin earth crust
resists less, thickened thrown highest;
stone, coral time evoke chitin's—
word time a voice bridled
as order, what is eternal

is living, a tree's growing
body's actual shadow in light.
Figured 135,000 years built up
from 75 foot depth the
coast gained from the sea—
upheaval subsided or still gaining—
colder currents south, warmer north:
conjecture not for the ganoid
or monkey dropped from branch's
perch—breccia—tumulus skull fished.
Cave, moraine—in peat moss
layers lie tree trunks, red
pine called *fir*, oak above
or beech; higher—alder, hazel,
birch sinking, aspen indifferently everywhere.
Summers looking across marches to
mountains an old mind sees
more, thinking of *a thought*
not his thought, older complexities:
the fractional state of the
annals, a bird's merrythought graving
of quill and down, apposed
human cranium's dendritical crystallizations offer
no sure estimate of antiquity
only archaic time unchanged unchangeable:
aeolian loess, glacier carrying *graywether*—
chipped and rubbed contorted drift—
concentric bed blue clay—white,
yellow sand, striped loam—blue
laminated. Laminated marl—fret changes
only himself, to prove peach
blooms, cherry blossoms, dogwood: seen
seeded flower; unaltered flowerless marriage
of spore. Races endure more
slowly than languages unconsciously sounding
skills as of bees in
a hive, animal passions range

human, alike their affections individual:
if created Once (*a thought*)
or thought of consecutively fossiliferous
marl saved froghopper, ladybird, glowworm,
red admiral, mingling in dredged
lake mud, anachronous stone, horn,
bone, jade, an armlet's brass
wire, flax plaited, not woven,
carbonized apple, raspberry, blackberry seed,
wild plum drupe, reindeer antler
nowhere, remains of a larger
hunting dog, a forest pony,
a burnt brick, and round
small bodies—fossils of the
white chalk—might have been
strung together as beads, the
bond that united them unbroken.
The departed celestial radiated alive
under earth rest will not
return above to hunger, sustained
by mayapple root, their children
unmolested fleeted by glowworms before
stars course ocean flicker continents:
north south west east uncompassed
only sun unshifting wind and
wave return drifted prow home
early sailors world no other
their earth's an island whether
hugged coast landlocked sea atoll—
lost on water discovery's accident
(with bat migrant at sea)
emerged from water nameless, story
celestial skin may help father.
Small wonder when they fish
some greet *food in water*
others count *one two many*
or for *forgiveness* hide in

noway able to think about—
unnameable things in their healing:
fireless cold tamed geese barren—
jackal, coyote ravished earth—separated.
Warming, blue ridge tore down—
rocks avulsed from their beds
water long percolating dripped caves'
massive columns, incrusted elegant drapery.
Where stone pillars leaned together
a smaller stone topped them
on furrowed plain—how plowed?
no iron, tawny-skin storied a
stick thrown to man, 'here's
an animal to follow you'—
this turned into a dog.
Faithful vivacity, pigmy and mammoth—
the difference of increment unsearchable—
sunned soil's son chyle fed
feigning stay a devout nothing
dog's letter growled dog-ear marked.
Dog his luck, stone passion's
tears, his mother sings, corn's
ground I may not hunt,
never lived without bringing some
thing fired, woven, hided, threshed—
water is mine speaking eddies
thru coiled shells, clouds trail
smoke hole—risen like millet
gone and come back—work
is by day; night's—don't
know, better than error, drums
weave two and dances shuttle
no new heart for an
old, old habit orders there—
sacred, knotted. Four for balance
deer born blue, rain trees
songbird pith: winding heartstring morning,

prosper, heal-all pays the fee.
A flat roof discerned area,
tread and riser how long.
Then trade thought of twins
both equally lovely, an ant
to witness while thing differed
with want each talked with
mouth true as the work
of hands that held it:
four eyes agreed birdprint wrote
for them—sun, weather *extol*,
metal say *chase*, wood say
carve, bone say *cut*—from
one place rayed or as
rainbow dispersed to each place,
in time lost white light.
As to flood, but for
You we'd all be fishes.
As to drought, why burn
a witch if she were
cause might make things worse.
Annals moon's summer midnight aerolite.
64 guesses at order in
mist early insatiate resigned to
the season, what's fortunate what's
calamitous creating created treads the
tail of a tiger and
it may, may not bite.
Stuck in a rut? try
a flagstaff pry the wheel
then horses may travel light
get on with less. Measure
(harmony) need not delight you
dwarfed pine still a pine:
sat until nothing was something
ancestral smile, 'empty, zimbabwe' knowing
not knowing everlasting. A roof

leader rains why be led—
he will take your sons
for war, and the fields—
king so part your supplement
fair kill's no valor in
uprooted valerian, belching his hymns
once yours. Seventy plants, thirty
trees cite the way why
argue it, those wise don't
inflict your living this place
simple, quiet, kind. The simplest
man laughs about greater intangibles
'it wouldn't be the way
otherwise.' Woo weigh not too much
less talk of "love" and
"right" raises what you bear
an infant grasp holds your
finger not its might, ice
melts, well-carved does not niggle.
Callous stone men great names
are too late if ties
are no ties cities feed ruins.
No songs where she's immortal
and if not no rites:
cosmos—it appears worlds—sphere's
peerless remove no side beside—
they see on and on
hear and do not breathe;
breath would be a soul's
allotted ills. At the most
truths dig caverns—pure water
drips, honey's yellow glosses figs
less sweet—calls bird-cherry mulberry.
Oaths obtrude on the silence
and a hero dotes on
a tale of honesty (beyond
ocean pillars on sand sun

goes over) of black and
white, gold stack for wares.
Times the gain from philosophy
hárassed: abuse—brothel and inn,
crueler out to look equal
to dynasties passing; high matter
rather harmless ignorance the spitting
seas redeem. No knowledge but
intimate pleasure, tho a trained
horse's no stone, takes trouble—
historic abstraction riffles his mane—
hoofs to bed disputing soul
owns laws' spiderweb surfeit's outrage,
wounds from acting in tragedies.
Pith or gore has 4
seasons, 20 yet boy, 40
young, 60 ripe, 80 aged
pursued pi beyond stratus, weights
and measures, the eyes doors
to sun, air thronged with
souls exacting heroes' crumbs, salt
from seas men with their
livestock dream, warned not to
pray, unsure where help comes
when Evening Star lowers to
Morning Star. How can you,
opinion's throbbing ear aimless eye,
serve ghosts—remain loyal, living
faithful glances, magic and medicine.
For *now* it is: *not*
is the same and can
be thought and thought is
now. Truth's way all one
where it begins and shall
come back again thru traceless
now the moving body's sphere.
Pride drenched faster than fire,

good laws uphold good walls
a breath up from the
sea—home, light upward silent
path to let others chatter.
Love and hate—souls of
animals and plants, where a
nest is tears may flow
no key to the tangle.
Mind would not defend itself
believing bone's of smaller bone
particle accreted elements—mind humble
before molten sun reflecting moon's
low fosses and far ranges,
a heaven of stones whose
swiftness made their separate orbits
one, that slackening would fall:
not justice nor virtue the
singer knew or life retraced
in annual holidays for boys.
A porter's neat wood bundle
talked wish, question, answer, command.
Our call's nature, sound is
shocked air, human virtue convention—
to which a pupil shrugged,
so crater fuses is that
all? most gorge to eat
I eat to live. Science:
a well—empty yet something
uncut; shadow speaking irks action.
Man featherless two-legs, at which
the cosmopolite plucked a fowl's,
'Here's your man—' *My teacher
gone mad:* 'loveliest—free speech'
(*unlicensed tongue*) 'true polity wide
as the universe, but the
great thieves lead the little
away.' *Your eyes see—prating—*

*not to my mind—expose
pride.* Like the Dog Star
set—died holding his breath.
Pragmatic *meaning equivocally* fare well.
*Trivial uttered, hard to stand
under:* polity's impossible without friends
and most want praise more
than health—by nature human
presence is not everlasting—speaking
for the good omen: against
chance perhaps some light sheds
nourishing itself seeing the need
without anger, without envy, without
stupidity—past speech, affectations, attitudes.
Air of early dawn, how
shun *jee* and *ch'*, eagre
bore the crest, o sun
if you die we do,
'if your house were burning
what would you save from
it?' 'The fire.' To see
small beginnings clear, the little
handicaps cause of a brood:
3 years on ivory leaves,
slighting green, leaves history poorer:
rejoic'd na *men* but *dogs.*
Earth, its people must weather,
but should *honor* plead *profit*?
Could do without the book
rather than read the ivory.
White snow, white feather, white
horse, is man white felling
hills for fuel, they revive
some shrubs, yet in the
early morning white hairs regret
the tree a child's heart
once grasped with both hands

concealing folly shrewd to age.
Esteem me now, may it
never happen to disprove any
to you the one love—
not small for the greatest
not great for the smallest
merely a tree's highest branches
fish happy water in water
what it is to be
water, butterfly or man know
stop by your own action:
there is the right moment
a feat standing, little earth:
knowing also the fishes positioned
whatever vector find purchasers, would
you have them suffer *justly*?
sometimes hearing a warning—learning
dam from the waters not
the sages, ancestors wore cotton
rot to growth, lore and
odor severe, planting useless if
the willows snarl a hull.
Annual in all parts annual—
mere regard won't carp, own
fruit sees his story as
defined, once understood by another.
With plants as with men
as to wild and cultivated:
cautioning fast and hard *definitions*—
poley sends moths from closets.
Some plants love wet: shore
trees color of roses, young
smooth bark, older rougher, vine
bark cracked, arbutus peeling, an
apple's animal faces. *Rooted*: felt
depth, density, core—distancing bare
ground the banyan roots from

shoots, roots again, no root
deeper than the sun's heat
reaches. A white fig mutates
to black, and the opposite
happens: replanted best with soil
it grew in or into
better. (Root cuttings *below* the
axil downwards!) Spines replace leaves,
the white poplars' turn their
under surfaces up and men
say 'summer goes' and as
leaves turn every which way
to the sun it's hardy
to see which surface is
close to the twig. Engaged
paroled of fate, we determine
nothing (not really) purvey their
idols, theories in no hurry,
ostensibly saying yes in fairness
to them (valerian purges itself)
suspend judgment (likely impossible) invite
calm as woods shadow, not
insensibly spared relatives, yet dusting
mementos shelter an older sister's
causes: walked alone and when
a cur leaped at him
just presence enough to accord
ruffled, *hard to defy human
weakness*, in a tempest saw
the little pig eat calmly.
'Why then study these things?'
'3 pennies for you who
need profit from learning.' To
translate the exile whose arch
eyebrows darken your thought, all
steel can achieve his songs
obviate, cuirass war-beard and ale.

Time vague gods intervals worlds
everlastingly themselves eidolons intellect garden
reading an old epic, cure
vacancy fills, returns profound inane
the sum total of things
does not vary, blest nature's
no backwater on life, free
as the need quicks thought,
fact apprehending main heads, duration
a knowledge that verifies—passion
may complain—wisdom most sensitive
to emotion can slow to
least hurt deepest pleasure, age
young in good things, and
young grow up without fear:
lampooned in off time by
a stage dancer restoring song
under scholia—'a schoolmaster physicist'—
attracting philosophers by fleeing them;
both deceived that humility exhausts
insolence. Nor will it do
saying, 'I desire neither profit
nor fawner, only my forbearance'—
few'll believe or allow you.
Scribes conceive history as tho
sky, sun, men never were.
In hard times the poor
politicize; in prosperous cheer the
prosperous: inflated state and abated
derelict pretend titular courage. Look
when shoe pinches East, about
the like era the same
need rouses West, the sum
of things does not vary
charged with the air everywhere
when fool sparks wisdom, shepherd
jailer, let the flogged escape

suffering innocence like you, kite
or phoenix, the date palm
bent: the law, water, shaped
to the container it's in.
Strength's perfection asks no prayer,
redeems every fault, dreams no
hell. Devotion cannot add or
subtract. The amiable spares both
the laughing and weeping *his*
rudeness. His integrity drinks is
sober, knows those who shun
pleasure greatly pretend, judged by
the fruit not the root.
Unpolished jade so hard steel
cut no scratch—traveler recorded
city shape of a chlamys,
street for men on horse,
library, harbor beacon: the mind
does not light of itself;
stripped to the meditated object
eyes, lights, out there here,
itself all ever, increate, seedless—
yoke fruits other, farming watercourse
brimming obstacle running by itself.
Temple altar light unextinguished *yes*,
sleep waylaid, mused more hours,
in a fire of coals—
bread: their past 5000 years
not duped by studied words
an idea meant a name
calls soul in me if
erased by drunken elephants or
ignored exile, born for fellowship,
no share, only all welcome
related by good nature, inviolable
adversity, ardor, actions animate rest:
their detractors modern late learning

a borrowed alphabet while children
counted 153 fish like sonnets.
Where they make a desert
call't peace: East penned stag's
more memorial for *who's who*
than a moneyed subscriber. Born
amoral seed, air as good.
Deemed tree–*who?* a bronze
tablet: ocean and teats: *scribe*.
Another: a husband and wife.
2000 years old: West-East dictionaries.
As tea guides this hour
keep, pear—her root's in
wrinkles: come now to practice
pressing me on, horse hear
us home, dismount is marathon.
May day assay the eyes'
chronicle light photos, chromatic fire
salt consumes animate? Enigma: tongue
gone scaling down sees apace,
clods deafmute let springs pray—
gay not drugged, sun raise
rarer air—unarmed little want—
wrist high unwearying bent, cosmos
fingers order trope to trope.
Choice by lot's no insight,
grass where his mother lay
can T any philosophical rambler
to a fist free of
theories, dotterel's last ties peridot.
To think His Thought: *Once*
(presumably) after Him: Delight, Tree
of the Sweet Fool's Utterance:
or later teaching a trodden
path: law—salt, water; restored
talk, story—wine, allspice. A
child learns on blank paper,

an old man rewrites palimpsest,
a good heart dejected brings
others peace, asks no returns,
assumes milestones guide all and
belong to each so no
one people can claim to
excel. Should wasp torture caterpillar
gait deprive ass of barley?
Do you come teaching from
your cave to destroy My
Earth's Fullness, return to your
tomb, who leads must run
there. Remember faith seeds, four
seasons celebrate, strength your girl's
summer her second time, her
wisdom given knowledge her purity.
How to write history, policy
an unteachable gift of nature:
farmer prophesies better than poet
two diapasons cleared mutes wrongs
nameless, "not mine" comes from
the sage calling fig *fig*
shown neither pity nor shame:
still with that flare on
horseback spurs its story afoot
never so overbearing or sure
entirely letters sealed with gypsum
shall when pharos crumbles reveal
"built for those at sea."
Or 6 nine's of material
light and fire from long
habit of greeting everyone, a
diffusion of warmth cold from
snow or flowers conceived scented
intimate in a whorl of
soul, received body always One—
its active Necessary unstopped modes

manifest of a source over
what change and chance bring—
unfaced and seeing all faces.
With two pupils to one
eye in the Eastern library
of 20,000 books one saw
the advantage of 4 tones—
a briefer cut to felicity.
Her lot among the poor
—a sacrifice of dough—rises
of itself: bread, not arrogance.
Different trees, different birds, different
songs, fish leap, float, mountains
rise, water dries, what for
who knows, when a doctor's
paradise does not run up
the price of his herbs.
Too full for talk, 4
tones of black glisten, healall
of black night, dark, light,
no more than a sound
can be painted, or wind
in the hollow of hand—
don't reveal for my sake
your church open for meditation:
dividing or returning actually, literally
He still is not, is
only as word to a
voice timed One in its
order to happen His singular.
Escaped conceptions clouds darken hang
without violence, orioles dart and
the rare flower opens, spring's
green snow the moon above.
Wistaria plights flute song unbroken,
Mayfly larvae launched rice husk
on sea. Three days rain

and the cold thank god
Who persists saying, *no*, nature.
Nature says, this wet, vine.
Centuries (place) telescope Sun rule
over star sea moon: ink
a Veery Coach uncreated creator
instructs Sun with His effects—
leading His slain dog immortal.
New knots renewed ink anew:
without wheel, coin—paved gold,
couriers mountain streams land tie
Sun's echo of song, innocence
works no need empire mines.
A goblet of prase, gems
shade light of a shrine
till a simplest mouth pierces
the meaning—the devotion of
craft ground fine before hero—
itself longs the taper right,
fare, light, for delight not
raising false hopes above nature,
miracle confirms only the possible
the eyes redeem while justice
monkies mischievous life, if she's
beautiful they'll see: action's end
is to finish. A beast
in a dream warns not
to kill in all languages:
maps, graved carved stones, musical
strings—blesses willow shoots shy
at dawn, still no buds.
Old scourge on whitenosed horse
you said pilgrims to *one*
shrine mistake sky's place *thruout*
earth. Gray tamarisk in black
wind survives you, no shrine
under your birthday tree lost

in thickening forest. White summit
of higher ranges hang golden
kaki, pomegranate that slaked thirst—
birds, conquered river take pleasure,
the boy's wise you said
his rose and pink flower
a deeper shade—gone timorous:
a single sunbeam enough to
drive away many shadows, *now*
stands still, not time beginning
to measure—verdant foliate pure
more mated. Brightness. Discriminates minutely,
eye looks to arch to
the Letter—Poverty the Fool's
Rod on his own back—
why deny what you've not
tried: read, not into, it:
desire until all be bright.
Called angelic instantly to resume
its humanity, it is not
enough to be happy: camel
suffers birth hardest—desert nomad
her midwife, few defiled names
resound again. Bought cheap, sold
dear—rite, high riser, alchemical
authority of men who'd make
men in alembic, consonants with-without
vowels quaver larynx and syrinx
rills work least with ideas—
history a plant that dies
tho the angel's messenger cry
war's trickery, forced labor's ruins,
gold's *not* the Prophet of
Work. Red-maple leaves a rush
of rich robes skyborne seamless
completed with breath of a
yawn what can divination teach—

venture here, venture lambent sidereal
foliage prevailing yet not impassable
new people's arrow weakens, call
us *ethereal gentlest,* birds echoed
this this November, their men's
magnanimity strips itself naked, each
stays, loves his first love:
needle's West seas urge East,
today shouldn't err, hard hearts.
Primitive: hurtless snail horn, painting
Order without Ordainer, cleaning ports,
troubled sea: virgule—a coach
seahorses draw home or one
dissonance winked conceived acting together
eyes fixed in their attention
even the stained wall vanquished:
one time the other: borne
with metal letters for all
nations, mirroring not with reed
penned notes lion chest opened
inventing lilies: if there's good
in sin depravation's hated, the
genial worse: let the deaf
judge with eyes, the blind
with ears, nearness and distance
motion and rest, the light
not limned by lines graces
face; the body figures, not
clamor, eddies of notes destroy
argument, eternize silence of stone
dim as it may—tell
me if ever—compare bones
of horse to man's tiptoe
Nailed eon in the second
hour a child knew better
asleep—for old age stone
thinks, judges no dust will
raise men of two mouths,

they spoiled the great world:
pitiful piety their fatuous fantasy
my art makes me their
idol: was there ever time
work did not convene endurer
modesty not cheap or foolish
a lovable woman's unpainted white
of her cambric forming her
landscape or portrait: confronted with
militia's tower ancient buildings stand.
Peaceable woods elude paradox desire
their uses thru the world
mine coals crystallize in earth.
Hats on scrape your boots
laugh it off, abstracter of
quintessence, speak mother tongue stonechat
click eternity cant love lacks
what it hasn't a Case
of One House—less ink
governing others, blind mole *perswaded*
any beast can see. Brained
mule, light heart, trumpet full
of vines mercy no merchandise,
art tracking music: loose as
the old beachcomber's gripe—*the*
folly . . craving for power . . circumnavigating
to read music into plumage—
eye den hearing—'hungry I
climb'd to eat grass'—envy.
In the flagrate of cold
theatre of the world the
wren and hindsight nest—an
architecture honors a people's obstinate
valor ages thru infinite changes,
cold, caldron run over, scattered
congregate, their sanctuary the Land:
the blood's motion—arteries to
veins and back to the

heart: come at last into
ample fields sip every cup
a great book great mischief
perched dwarf on a giant
may see horse race or
hidebound calves out to pasture:
poet living tomb of his
games—a quiet life for
an ocean: *the emphatical decussation
quincunx* chiasma of 5-leafed, 5-
blossom, and of olive orchards
5 fingers of a hand
crossed X of bird merrythought:
conjugal or wedding number: all
things began in Order to
end in Ordainer, yet always
few genera rule without exception,
make their worst use of
time's shortness conceding the fletcher's
mark—*our ballads care little
who makes the laws:* the
higher geometry dividing a circle
by 5 radii which concur
not to make diameters: not
necessary that the things a
sceptic proposes be consonant,
only that the abler speak
plainer, solid as the illiterate
seeing water boiling, hissing at
the ends of burning logs:
to fare soul not bothering
my son's the world paroles
with words, pleasing Justice—
a meridian decides. *To guard
the glories of a face . .
the senses are too gross
and he'll contrive a Sixth
to contradict the other Five—*

still the same as each
other without loss of truth
life knits: Health's one Thing,
moving the Earth . . a proposal . .
Ox world needs put on
the Furniture of a Horse . .
who can make Shadows, no
thanks to Sun? 4 tones
teen blood's tide to think
or panser, dress wounds or
groom. *No, one cannot play
everything at first sight* (Old
Peruke—*Sir, a piper?*) Hardly
hell wit's use: *I prefer
people say* 'it isn't so
crazy as you might think—
we're different species.' An historian's
vindication: *minute particulars of little
moment to whom they belong*;
doesn't *pretend to have read
all Authority . . factions . . disturbed happiness
in this world for the
sake of the next . . request
they forget my vindication.* Bawling
inhuman unison—*study affinity*, ciliate
animal strains—*the angel philosophizes
paths bordered with nevergreen.*
Scrimshaw: taste bud savors go
of a thing—mort trumpets
whale has its louse—the
tragic multiplies farce; value is
simple, heartened in water crystallizing
pure crystal, cóntent beyond phase.

Between grape bay and hungry
bay wind song and sea
foam, reef (stone beeves)—struck

green kelp waves arms, dips
tons my only eyes fear:

merely—ocean blued windows sweat
between soused bitten cliff and
that—we're freed by silence,
anger lights windflower, tears': or
a mad gist always glad?

sun burns thru the roars
dear eyes, *all eyes*, pageant
bay inlet, garden casuarina, spittle-spawn
(not laurel) nameless we name
it, and sorrows dissolve—human:

behind terrace boat plant under
back wall pear tree hugged,
its twigs paired axile thorns
crossways opposite leaves thought quincunx
urged all day in town

walked past wild narcissus of
another cottage areaway, fan palm's
purple date across the road
downhill to lily-turf (snakebeard—Once)
shag bordered arboretum banyan, shadow

rooted above ground—mazed alien
gazeless stare seeled pulse. In
town mid-ocean shoppers, fiscal lunchers
at the marina breezing, discount
banking an obstinacy of continuity.

Idlers of extinct volcanic island
thinking quincunx when a flash
hurricane bid early tea—trees
undiscerned from sea exemplified them
comedians bowing out of the

theatre incommoding others, 'that was
quick . . drying'—birds homing twilight
the arboretum plants light green
only against darker, darkest green
lumens of viburnum, sea-fig aloe—

(be my gardens to be)
uphill one road-shoulder lower, night
haste, first heavenly dark, wind
and the roar louder divining
boat plant and pear tree

behind the door—the cable
thought shuns thinking ahead of
grief waited: better not see
death as *every body goes,*
sister . . beyond the laboratory brain . .

that alive longed for friends,
had's misery's not to have
when our lack enjoins them
death vying with their lives.
Another place, another time: timeless.

Mist, summit disembodied lake, moonlighter
hours a ferry ghosts the
pier: these our actors . . Ayre . .
it isn't true 'if I
met that voice I'd die

of fear'—too easy said,
rather fear should die: a
good hour's wait then color—
peaks, snow, red, sapphire, prase
Leo'd hear again 100 forearms

perpendicularly fuming milk noise down,
ride horses look straight between

their ears, do like the
man next to you, resurrect
ruins: two-branch lake looks up:

higher than the belvedere the
promontory heads past terraced ledge
fief rockfalls into higher woods
sun-snowgust gales' interchange flowers favor
on New Year's: black hellebore

(or winter rose) white literally
(botanically not a rose) leaves
evergreen almost stemless entwined in
rocks' creviced snow: ages gently
a peasant gardener's attentions, blossoms

he greets by ancient names
'iberis prefers limestone—evonymus prospers'
no twenty-two reasons argue them—
unurged aptness untallied sunned the
comedy's divine, tragic a Thought:

a nerve's aching respond to
energies not itself: old in
a greenhouse the stabled horse
sings sometimes, thoughts' template
somehow furthers a cento reading:

oval stairs, diminished steps, wings
either side . . in my mind
a dream of named history
content with *still-vext Bermoothes . . where
once thou call'dst me up*

. . to fetch dew . . tears: *there
she's hid* an arm embraces.

"A"–23

"A"-23

An unforeseen delight a round
beginning ardent; to end blest
presence less than nothing thrives:
a world worn in whose
happiest reins preempt their histories

which cannot help or hurt
a foreseen curve where many
loci would dispose and *and's*
compound creature and creature together.
Each lamp casts its shadow

after its lampshade—concentric—flared-
flower—hurricane chimney—midnight blue
hair of intermittent allayed water
most of such gossamer scarcely
moved in spirit to word

what hurries? why hurry? wit's
but the fog, the literal
senses move in light's song
modesty cannot force, blind call
its own, nor self-effaced fled

to woods perpend without pride
stone into lotus. The least love
lasts, the troubled heart foregoes
its sigh . . upon a time . .
going a way is here

as if a child sings
a li'l bit of doggy
heaven, teased by nestling eyes
of white little furry cat
their toy fascination of lazulite

crystal, sunlight of sunlight, older
desire chances naming, thought smiling
*no more than hungerpang aged
eating cures*: it persists, acts
whiteness with—without—sweetness or

invoked *equisetum—horse + bristle
(field horsetail)* research won't guarantee;
tongues commonly inaccurate talk viable
one to one, ear to
eye loving song greater than

anything—unhappiness happiness moves too
susceptible, and in extended world
where does the right thumb
throb—how far from a
room's wall, from its floor—

impelled necessary fingers respond to
when the face looks (*immobile*
to onlookers, ignorant shifting prejudgment)—
unhurt, near as three trees
growing together hush one heart.

Neither can bent hobnails flung
chance's play equated aleatorical notes
hurt public oblivion, no more
than skiddaw rock emitting tones:
the sea is our road

the land for our use,
damp cannot warm the houses—
linden thrives, one minute of
blue and sun then downpour—
treecolumned greensward greener, man empty

spaces in cells sounds thick
gardens, digs up, plants may—

stem climb clockwise, counter-, sage
spirals, lavender curls, burgeoning wind
sing root hurried lower skirt

entombed coppers—merry-go-round, riding ridden
merry-go-round root: from where sipped—
constant rubric handle sun jut
rose cold—blood's ebb initial—
from steep mountain courtesies in

seconds flames upper half what
submerged name in coldénia, second
paradise turnsole suns again, borage
corolla clear blue, anthers sapphire
after a night thinking sun

towing of earth on earth:
dwarfed mimosa has shut—sleeps:
flood'll lull nations windrows: oak-ilex
holm: the rushbottom chair legs
shortened accord seat and back

cushions—2 crewel threads flowers,
1 worsted thread animalcule or
purposely minimal armed goddess caressing
the floor—wholeness over broom—
her logic's unanswerable refurnishing from

nothing: unstopping motion whose smallest
note further divided would serve
nothing—destined actual infinitely initial,
how dire his honor who'll
peddle nothing: rendered his requiem

alive (white gold-autumn-leafed mat cut
down to 1-foot circle and
tasseled) would praise when 80

flowers the new lives' descant
thought's rarer air, act, story

words earth—the saving history
not to deny the gifts
of time where those who
never met together may hear
this other time sound *one.*

Ye nó we see hay
io we hay we see
hay io we sée no
we see knee (windsong bis)
we knee we see hay
io we hay we see
hay io we see knee
hay io wé see knee
hay io we hów we
see hay io we see,
no wee knee no wa—.
Akin jabber too hot to
rail all but cheek a
hard game clambers treed, cliff
for honey has she danced
ahead there, pipes and flute,
let her dance ahead (5-year
planner plans a wife, nose
whose now he knows) papyrus
jungle sandhill splayed-wedge wader damsel
crane: or sun hot bright
turn home slowed yellow horse
or cold with fear the
need turned small sing itself—
font of old white cloud
and men grown flower plough
empowers how soon their senate

night debate proves mixed blessing
to a wife up late
child's tears years o la
la lu, rocked raring horses
sue myrrh holy leazing golden
tile. Praise! gill . . gam . . mesh . .
excellent body sunned whose world
journey wore out His wisdom
building: wall God and Goddess
copper-crowned cornice under Firmament . . foundation . .
terrace . . masonry . . proved fired brick
magus tier, temple—One Kid,
a hillgazelle, unsprung trap, stopped
pitfall, freed beasts to eat
grass *with* them, spurned Strongest's
rite 2/3-God (only 1/3-man) on
the young herds' bridal night—
one simple innocent crying *I'm*
stronger in Strongest's dream: "*Mother*—
dreaming blessedly such stars' wealth
my people with me a
meteor fell we worshipped, you
foresaw him my brother, *need:*
Mother—dreaming on I loved
him above harem, my belt-ax—"
"Stronger, your friend I've foreseen"
"My lot who sháll be."
Strongest sent, his harlot went,
One Kid exulted until unmanned,
returned together dry, Stronger craving
Strongest's close friendship—*his* need—
one simple innocent crying *I'm*
stronger bragged understanding wrestling until
The Strongest threw him: their
friendship sealed. Strongest to Stronger:
"my heart weighs my lot,
if 2/3-God must die weal's

37

beyond rancor; evil's unfinished I've
seen myself corpse bloat, river
flood-water surge my Wall—búoyed
no more than any urbanite;
hated I desire the forest—
risk to come thru it,
daring will reach my father
have him in unmeasured Distance
avow us brothers, like Him
everlasting." Stronger wept, heart against
going: "fated, Strongest, deal justly."
"Stronger fears me?" (Later he
agnized: rejected son supernal being—
horse in massed water, soaring
star.) Entered the Forest—friends:
(decalcomania) madness trampling The Spirit,
Its Seven Cedars, Stronger lopping
their crowns, fagoting till It
misted, "Spare me, hack treemountain
instead for a palace." And
Stronger: "Don't, not to be
Strongest now's fatal"—together uprooted
cedarforest till moonrise luring a
Goddess: "Strongest, marry *me*." He:
"What dowry do you crave
to seel me worthless, who's
had your unfailing love—the
wailing herd, the roller-bird tumbled
k'-k', the 7-ditched lion, the
stallion muddied whipped, Your Father's
gardener charmed mole?" She raged,
grappled, Stronger harrowed, hers—Strongest
sobbing, "Why you, not me
dying," his friend reliving, coma
cursing trapper and harlot, "O
Stronger, why do you curse—
I dreamed you—my désert

's real before me." Stronger
ashamed—awake one instant—heart
stopped. A veil for Strongest's
friend, as veils a bride:
weep 7-Days, 7-Nights, Stronger's deaf—
given to earth and worm.
A hardwood table, two bowls:
carnelian blushes honey, sapphire swims
butter in sunlight for Stronger,
sapphire breast in gold body
becoming his monument. Strongest mourns,
"Like him I shall be
dust vanish unless my father
everlasting—stirps my wander seeks—
make me so and my
friend brothers everlasting together: while
Stronger cannot rest in me,
how can I destroyed destroying?"
Dark tolling, deprived echo, Strongest
tunneled 12 leagues of treemountain,
rages into whelming sun—hedges
flower carnelian, bud sapphires—quests:
"Everlasting Garden yet death smell
mine still quick to sunlight"—
bayed fury strayed to seacoast.
In closegrapearbor a veiled girl
turned away. But he: "I'm
Strongest." And she: "Hurrying? Whereto?
Beyond you that's never? Better
a bath's clean linen, the
glad wife embraced, a child
fondling you: the common lot
prizes its days' night sleep,
risks less. How sure's destroyed
sailing dead sea only sun
crosses not asking everlasting pity?
Still obdurate, asking? Well: your

father's pilot-in-the-woods ferries that sea.
Failing sail home age harvesting."
Incorrigible Strongest destroyed the woods'
holy stones for the crossing,
rebuked flawed the pilot's ire:
built a new boat, sailed
him 3 days more like
40—sudden landfall, timeless sunrise
blazing mountain blindfolded in them—
Everlasting distantly awaiting them—asking:
"No tackle or mast what
haggard human in beastskin dare
steer my pilot-in-the-woods with him"—
seeing his son, "offcourse or
windlull?" Strongest: "a dead friend . .
despair . . asking you raise us
anew together perpetually brothers." "How
can I, fatal. Eternal's forever,
everlasting came after, and no
part-fulness contracts forever. Or
it's as you look: only
the dragonfly's unformed wings wait
the sun for its glory.
I outlived a flood to
be called everlasting, to know
distant partings of tidal river,
asleep and dead grow alike.
Take home my gift, my
secret, the plant you shall
name, this journey as under
water, '*Alive-Old-Stay-Young.*' "
Sog's freighted, o sod hear,
whisper, rain, think men unashamed—
your minds no risk—divine
dawns' daughters prolong th'years go
sounds fearing no rued palm.
Sheer laud anew sheer chorus

sheer laud new, call our
race, allay shadow th'woods hear:
poled any mouth pant keep
pace, come back *who says*—
tribesettled cosmos, pigmy, a sea
clangor rŏw-on of cranes—order,
loveliness, universe not improved upon:
mills' crop yellows ground, hoy,
how they foresee full-lone nakedness—
wind argue row of blackpoplar
leaves—strove o seen: orchards
4-acres, 4-mornings ploughing, tree sap
tying winter into summer. Hue
gait a day—by new
sill a rose pause seen—
nape—horse whose tizzied head
o my—lip own anatomy
the oak I. Trivial uttered
hard to stand under, crave
touch gently gray springtime allotted
all ways, zones know eager
echo argue less daimon in
ere thigh rote tone eroded—
and deem a phase shine,
died corona come as may.
In us laces you, hot
ay happy fire triumphant, triumphant
sate your health, chased sea
moons feed our leave to
return: all you live—near
him, sap pay rue if
near him, live near him
if near him, low door
a har: eager atone the
tie—voice to eye, sun's
two doves' highway's shadow moves
up from earth—chimeras' horses

marry: a whole tear glee
would seem rain lashes dam—
young years weave old looms.
Cut your harvest old lashed
giver, how many may make
charred roots: why you goad
loved weed loam more than
harm'll frame (why) whom now
winds' woodpeople move, rue, ache,
choir shocked call rest, pause
renew—whirligig punning tempest, cut
sere harvest: massif, I saw
my honed knife, hearts' myriads'
shawm call anew: *till, hymn*:
rosy-lea, rosy-lea, o lea bought-dim—
in fire root us: horses'
drivers free, right heart, dolphin
hours ride, float wrist-held wrist
belay who moved dim tears
upon them: island sings spreads
a swimmer's hands whose flowers
'd fill worlds new, o even
when his couch's shorter than
his story, his coverlet his
skin robbed, aim show white:
sitfast: a time as no
mismade hymn: wholly see—call
the gay hymn nothing—efface.
Akin: grass: peoples a veil.
Each nameless allay: grass' showers.
Head look my toe—justice,
we have it *graced*, who
hasn't lagged modestly looking alone,
the end a good note—
saw dwellings prophecies turn back
the eyes. Anthem th'new meadow:
rhododendron, crocus-eye color violet, white

hyacinthine narcissus' own, dole on
the most tone: gone o
onto their—Doorstone see grace
so proffer own he met
her on, acclaim's own sun
go new *on. Rector of*
ox-stealers (May's born) *a*
varied finger, tortoise tasting th'
odoriferous grass, means to live
love-thee-ever, virtuous his home contént:
inform'd a lute twinklings' eye
rich (off and on and)
apt to learn—sought out
integrity, desire to light up
reverencing *with his soul the*
Sun to all Earth's sweetest
air exposed, reaps infinite acres
a new voice lording swindle
house-break, shop-lift—a song worth
50 cows. "*Ho, old man!*
you grub those stumps before
they will bear wine? (old
animal, no Dogwood shaft) *Attend*
advice: Seeing, see not; hearing,
hear not: and—if you
have understanding, understand."
(His gain mother earth—pant
on—I sum it up)
happy (when) *glory invests his*
sons fit means to live:
when the sun's evening horses
down, to stand its rise
some time his own. Agave:
key ever she'll rule, her
mirrored glory hold him, blow
away evil—what better prophet
or profit late rains' gale

may say why the canna—
piece it there's no peace—
voice call your eyes: call
days *so shone* seem cheer,
call bridegroom call bride—heats
tree's roots to the river
and the leaves remain green
first born a watered garden
return with their whole love:
who knew his faithless heart
will love not teach his
nearest, know each faith faithless
when nearest *might* be nearer:
be constant distance, least windflaw
forming the leaves: *mean* 'no
shame'—that is 'blessed' sun
for a light—old, ordinances
of the moon, stars. (Short
view) streets razed—who chose
no heir old scion cross-wise
(shriek hymning gain, raked birds
without cause all imaginations wrath)
stove labors youth's been thru?
Hush seeking oath now go
brightness pass you, high hill
lifted hand water anointed rush—
the labour of the olive
horses walk thru, the sun
moon stood, singer stringed instrument.
Spirit: wheels whirring forward unmoved—
water by measure 1/6 hin
bread-must now sheep ptomain: key—
a maker's mime-core'll show void
by crying: a little sanctuary
my people one heart (enemy
wall men vermillion—no gods
that slay) each one's vision

act wherever scattered'll know a
prophet lived once (against despite)
paired hedge with gap in
the Land in her Height:
comae of her branches over
days outcasts that need wandered
return a sheaf (from terror
cedar could not hide, Tall
and Skill all how many
cut off underground *slept* their
swords under their heads) Gate
of the Outward-Court looks North
3 little rooms to each
3 windows their arches and
palm-tree antae, measured like the
Gate looking East, approached by
seven steps its arches THERE,
an inner court by the
South Gate, arches toward the
Utter, going up to them
eight steps. The building at
an end of a secluded
space West, glory shone East
sunrise a threshold, heated sound's
ebb of water to sea,
guddled runnels swerved nearer blossoms
each month thru the year
child—stranger's like your own
none uprooted the heritage HERE.
Your nest among the stars . .
peace . . flame . . fields . . BRANCH . .
a thought not your thought
. . wholeness . . tracing see into grain . .
Is it to fast an
houre, Or rag'd to go,
Or show A down-cast look,
and sowre? No . . a Fast

45

to dole Thy sheaf of
wheat . . to fast . . From old
debate, And hate: thy life . .
a heart grief-rent . . Heart's nubile
trees, wordless, horses draw from
the isles new earth . . not
desolate . . from new moon . . another . .
rest . . sowers-wage-rages . . harassed nations . .
good *will* covet, desire redeem:
'I have loved you, yet
you say *wherein.* Return, I
return' A coast unseen.
By the river sat down
remembered the harp on the
willow required a song a
song in a strange land
the score a right hand
the back of a tongue.
'Child where father.' Oppose pomp,
rain, go on in peace.
Out hale as pole-loose horse:
look up, horse, a voice
foregoes a light it generates—
happy, fond, again as seen:
a gaze hailing a suitor
(cobbler) me, eye net *I*
quoin own me; lest we
lose a common cure anew
there loo pace aching feet—
my mother 's Harmony: whispered loves.
Who's *not* dead pan a
better way. One basket: scoop,
sifter and cradle: barley-and-oat-
born, a "goat" for spelt—
that quicked vestigial cycles' glomerate
horrid-eyes, pawn own none—agon
of self-sown rye—who's thru

part-rush, sick gone, leg on
bruiting doves phantasm unwinged pleading
wailing the labor upholding sky:
you mean a day's grace
stand to *day* I'm beside.
Back (*bach*) high: streaking. Be
kind, kindred don't phone in
your deaths—my *promise sure*
won't phone my own. *Babai!*
pent ooze beat brook, earth
its zone, pineflaming chorus pursue
a round, gods not body
in a skin the insane 'd
withe with refractive bee wing
to haircurling fury—compassion settling
foolishly dotes: gold leaf, mad
strength—best one sure friend:
gods nap alone or core
a loss so loom as
auras their race coils serious
heir solemn as their own.
Maker—hard breaks his syllable.
Tesserae Graces—you Fourth out
here The Three are Graces:
próchoös hand pours seek a
lane to sing odes, bird-praise
to cabinet-rasp, bow-drill, fine file,
semblance of two-headed hammer flogging
sieves emblazed suns, Cypress hidden
sky-starred bema, god egg-candled
kindling—falling toward—earth cypress,
at one with the hill-genius
wistaria cloaked, ivy girded smiling
lost in azalea, fallen meteor,
vine winding in twisted laurel
elbows wintering green—naming gazes
on undergrowth berry *I'm hers—*

profiting children with song whose
laws are another time veiled
timeless, consoling the aged reading
of a past meeting sorrow,
'pine, wherever your hanging garden,
my prince, comb our hearts—
as soft pine-needle your hair.'
Quasi poet quire repair to
men, elude—where's his similar:
tan hallow tan glow can
allay, mix lips summon eye,
burn cold, sob by sea—
floated head drowned others drowns
tree-haft wields ax, redeems captivity
a minim worth—th'pine'll
free her, cane, mossed hurdles,
arbutus wicker—outwitted outwit a
sea put to't, pear, nubile
illumine, *not smoke of flame,*
light from smoke to giue
.. *and in ther time*: humus
humider flowers: candid lily carpet,
no scanter violet, rosebud rime-matted
imperative purple's furious calyxes.
Imbibe the clepsydra, blue charioteer
nose offend a more ambulant
scene "what cracker deafs our
ears"—as to what rarest
temper reads our matter, post
fate her time-veined glory, kin
air too late (no proper
grief would attest its dole)—
censure plays, faults nameless who'd
"love" her "kind" autograph of
bookstóre remainder given free, but
is she worth such *poor*
taste? Molest your hand? no—

fake and go. Without clamber,
bunt, our book's *my own*:
delight seen one time: so:
married *once*: mirrored fire admired
animal probities father risk. Keys
punt: arbors tutor us: air
is, *air* is, short or
long sounds air's measure. In
toga—chord: release—pine, dewed
olives, damn papyrus, method, blot
of famine. Cart a new
case: fritt'll lose? Stave lucre.
Surge to breakfast bakery's pattycake,
birds tackling crust sound *look*,
kiss: Aves: inexpert hum quests
(tacet) statuary brume mutes acre
reclaimed. Terrace marring acclinate tide—
quiescent and to go on
(how, perturbed, pray happier). *some . .*
served . . ther cities . . altering . . the
sons arising place . . So to
ourselues we bride an air
clear, a ligh and brethe . .
What . . imparte . . to the? . . silence . .
suafes thing . . forget the yl.
History our arm script oars?
cresset? mule to damn nose
or papyrus: animal buss abstained
legumin: humane, A Thought Worshipped.
Or thrall a lull sing
swallows dawn weave *Crabbed age*
and youth . . together. Feast *. . eies . .*
Short night to night, and
length thy selfe to morrow . .
THE PASSIONATE PILGRIME . . through the
veluet leaues the wind . . the
learned man . . the Lady gay . .

For then . . song ended. Night
round Day *on*: post qualm
phoebe-phoenix: scent: too frigid dims.
Vagabond "stars" hale old windjammer
into a stone theatre dispute—
"you'd dispossess shanty and garden
claim tillage arrears, buried monies,
crowd rats with your men,
who buries money doesn't sprout
seed? Sun's ebongold shadow in
his eyes boy-ox'll crave, afford
hymeneal, find face haired eyes-ears-kiss,
unseasonable reasonable peril (peoples stone
lifelong) trothplight names later: Peace—
Place Whose Streams—unregretful minds
always sense roses, grape, clematis
twine rage ridge of porcupine."
Loyal . . *extrauagant* . . *erring* redeems infernos
'gainst that Season comes . . heard
. . in part beleeue it . . is
as the Ayre . . Walkes o're
the dew. Naked at birth
naked in earth reads *wrath*
illumined, 'took' (ay) down a
tone: Fortune's Temple Miss-Fortune's Tavern
nation smoked-cheesecake, Awe together deterrent.
Long years cellarer flatters no-one—
pursuing daimon. Melée he's daimon—
agog o league a-god ran-on.
Ai need's *ane* hárassed stone.
Young name grew old, older
names another: hermit yoke shuns
trafficked humility. Mudguard beggars mud,
a hermit cloud creates itself—
none knows me, why rankle:
. . man's life's . . to say "One."
Substance foreárms shadow: plants freeze

50

and thaw "naturally." Shadow confides:
disembodied when shadowed, in sunlight
together. Substance breathes, thinking:
whose praised virtue is sure?
Let be . . a time perceives
with *all readiness* . . pitched high
ridgeplate (kingpost roofed) one's eavesdropping
secret—fenced and the chainlink
spring's locust blossoms alight on
discóurse, 'none impressed none oppress':
unsighted uses 7 or 8
small rooms to ramble in—
looking within, listening out windows:
a dog's nosing bark lifts
starlings: scattered choir less. East:
the old mulberry's escapes, wild
locust, 5-lobe-leaf maple honeysuckled to
an outgrown rhus (woodhouses . .)—as
the eyes turn North lilac
blue-red, white too, right-angled facing
stone porch whose low wall
ranges (pachysandra mingling) yew, flame-azalea,
box-like shrub holly, kalmia more
you, discolor willow with the
lilac. West—from windowed bays,
trimmed hemlock halves each—hills,
at the road's three-crossings to
them evenings candle chestnut blossom
candles ten times the life
of the watcher's hat, question
bird migrant promises nest there,
respond of South windows: in
the ground ivy half a
house-wren's egg pink-white as the
slingshot by: spring's ant wings
and (under stones) runs a wake
to a song mostly chrysanthemums'.

Regal mien swathed unrustling tread
o'the wick, búoy, waded reef—
willing my habit overhailed-ayre beat,
wrest-pins lifting me welcome strung
guest into cloud over folk,
flood, fold (and my name?)—
these lift, bear, little over
barrow lighted: cinder black with
swart sallow body. Songs rove
heap'm fare rath loud chirm
tread at barnhouses 'll hum poor-souls
knit to bairn now name
themselves—'starlings.' *ait, aight, eyet,
eyot, eyght* sing *the same*
. . river . . among green aits . . *eye-land*
islands and meadows. A laugh . .
and not butt my head.
Claque-law—bard hard, fire yet:
miracle porker-lane, apple, birch, greetings:
calf-eyed, pie betide thee . . gore
off head a great delight
beguile war in the nightingale—
lullaby to your bounty, lulla
tree, snow-lee—eyry air goad.
Flute, feather stridor, horse-scamper; beggar
clown-sage, love-must know dessert desért
(earth's ring bare knee . . ice . .
ness . . tempest . . "not Green-land" . . sigh
and Wine-land woodleaf *sprag,* eyed
create sky-fires—be roof and
do know my like 'll home—
who knows *one* . . all alone
3 the fathers, 4 the
mothers—9 to birth) my
dove 'll echo . . of guide-ruled sleep . .
be a Shown ware eye
given to waylay fear: m'core—

fountain: by *heart-strings* 13 frets
propound a law of 'all'
and each fret tuned singly
salves fret or singularly frets
to salve thing to End
dissonance harmonized: Its temple's second
evening weeps, *'this bane above'*—
the third morning praises, 'shoregrass
dances, *finished!' This bane abhorred
betrayed and sold hod, god-yowl—
One Kid a gad 2 sou
sloughed Death.* As wide the
Land (*so gret feith* . . could
have her sob or sigh)
who throws his forces no
stray way benign his mother
quests; 'munch it, long eyes
dote, hance *stamped the leasing*,
demurrer's infant's fear—swinish the
fish, night—a long time
to zee, the rush of
fountain clears . . *lots to blanks* . .'
'Sober toes soul's reveller solaced
trope in-their-midst,' 'blazed, man, trove-airs
occlude sots, grant chant's precise
that's its praise—none "equal," touch'
(Chicken manure petrol, old man
of tot ness, the far-out
least poison . . the waste . . the
perfecting machine corrupt within)
'Time may't please hear her
voice praise *good* all th' sum—
loved th' dull core rabbet and
dowel' 'a lent tear air'
'gardened from grand gulf marred.'
Rock . . oak not wind-shak'd surge
wind-shaken mane, cast water, on

the burning Bear . . prefers truth
doubt, not reason what's hidden—
felling hymn, dispersions, chords collect
grow, unmar wit, air East,
seconding heart-chords' dictate (mane 's crier,
sum professes). Patience diligence seek
her, flute woodnotes forbid enthymemes,
sorites 'talk no rule to
nerve fires sear: wolf hungry
daimons are her Fool-pauper's wardens
widowed child of th'heathen': *their*
chores little adventures across grasses
tax no thatch for barrack
wardrobe, booksack—one long shirt
—no wallet—'ll do. You spoke
for me of *my* cell,
I'll not work its silence
and peace again—now anybody's
sloth to stretch in, psalter
and breviary: ashes, I a
breviary better lug stone. 'Love
more, come follow another's region
or—' '(if) light's inchoate inform'd
sphere rendered its matter powerless,
rarefaction actual as 1 all
numbers follow, in Earth's mother
the superior luminaries collect ever
as bodies.' 'Guide, o were
a star seem us 1'
'We cannot meet so the
false Spirit fly, leave thee
thy integrity' 'Null all true,
see chanting, trust descant scaling.'
Lightnings redder than reddest stallion
whither lamp crier this glare
can willow man look April-eyed
silver clasps and rings mercy'n'

lewd gold mop his sister's
hair this ghoul fool ogling
up-on a rouncy as he
couthe, The firste stok, fader
of gentilesse . . the firste fader
in a summer season when
soft was the sun Unholy
of Works went wide in
this world wonders to hear
swayed so merry field full
of folk the mean and
the rich bidders and beggars
gone high to bed: the
common contrived locked up a
lunatic a lean thing winkle
allays, cried then *hot pies*
hot good grease and geese.
Terrainal paradise's consolation, solace will
agree years improve her salutation.
An album-leaf: on the Hill
together looking down children crisscrossing—
'misunderstood stung vanity almost the
same points from different directions
approached afresh the same
desire speaks' 'not for them
but with them, prest lips
voice the bent dray-horse, pack
illumined sweat-light, hair grows long
fern-mane rises, ears-ringing words start.'
Of Nought—light, leaf, grief—
lend grace wife and her
son keep to life's end
serein (horse) a full lawn.

An art of honor, laud—
'pleasures do' wit's joys accord:

57

so on hand-vowed integrities, unaltered
syllables, the fended wrist, fires'
light rest: bourne eyed 'll guide
gar them hear draw ear
brute dear úp-on a rouncy
aske nomore . . go. Clear honor
liquid element, dull th'arroyo, codas—
rising: repeated, sun's a comet
to string a kit with
(sheep feint a bee hue-new
pulverable enamour'd) 'one body's resurrection
not half so great as
one flown grain uprising wheat'—
'seek gloss hours fáre on'
'structure a winding stair at
two removes,' oneself, all *selves*:
frond then tagging silvers—increate
garden only first hour thatch
reading earth's scripture, while a
star knows yew vinted lower
trysts weave, the sheep happier
without the care of wolves.
West redskins' talk grammars older
than East's. Tongues: lark's wings:
'*hi*!' requires a serious answer
agglutinative questions when no redskins
lust white gospel in red-tongue.
O my dear Ms Tress
don't it know . . naturally . . Pride . .
Daughter of Riches . . the Republick
of Dogs . . the Many . . usurps
sympathy, salted hurt—cutting off
feet wanting shoes. *Fame's fib,*
sweetness and light, hummed the
bee, *whale-of-a-swale two hearts one*
case—argute mute: inventive? no,
had seen a man High-hill'n

front, warm woods back—grig
ling, furze, gorse, fern. Let
Bee-sting hold back, the flowers
arrive she nurtures them—waggery,
gravity (patience upon approbation) can
creep for the flower-of-a-leaf—
man and earth suffer together:
two centuries touching cold-ridge inventoried
abreast of '10 years—80 flowers':
Jubilant agony too too sped
dive-dapper peering through a wave
. . another way . . pied-billed grebe, rock-nerve . .
eye against a lamp-post—eh—
. . in each heart . . that punctual
servant of all work, th'sun
tones: Hunting! ho city stone:
labours clocked though it 'strikes,'
ale's sorrow cheer poured, diddled
ebony Images whose 'nigritude offends
we mean to gild'em' 50
truths to a false conclusion—
diplomatpatriots slaveryribbons in lapel buttonholes.
Good thoughts in bad times:
sane genius violent undreamt judgment
devouring 'blades' wilding gentle—angel
in barber's hands—never less
alone when alone has lit
up the hated things taking
more space than their worth
"politic reasons whore"—the brain
has its weakness, comment'll craw—
stolen apples spur running—he'll
forget his rote is his
in unbreath'd pleasure sometime: race
no protest . . wise . . provident . . reach.
A living calendar, names inwreath'd
Bach's innocence longing Handel's untouched.

Cue in new-old quantities—'Don't
bother me'—Bach quieted bothered;
since Eden gardens labor, For
series distributes harmonies, attraction Governs
destinies. Histories dye the streets:
intimate whispers magnanimity flourishes: doubts'
passionate Judgment, passion the task.
Kalenderes enlumined 21-2-3, *nigher* . . *fire*—
Land or—sea, air—gathered.
Most art, object-the-mentor, donn'd one—
smiles ray *immaterial Nimbus* . . *Oes*
sun-pinned to red threads—thrice-urged
posato (poised) 'support from the
source'—horn-note out of a
string (Quest returns answer—'to
rethink the Caprices') *sawhorses silver
all these fruit-tree tops:* consonances
and dissonances only of degree, never-
Unfinished hairlike water of notes
vital free as Itself—impossible's
sort-of think-cramp work x: moonwort:
music, thought, drama, story, poem
parks' sunburst—animals, grace notes—
z-sited path are but us.